First World War
and Army of Occupation
War Diary
France, Belgium and Germany

9 DIVISION
3 Lowland Brigades
Royal Scots Fusiliers
1/4th Battalion.
1 April 1919 - 31 August 1919

WO95/1776/11

The Naval & Military Press Ltd
www.nmarchive.com
Published in association with The National Archives

Published by

The Naval & Military Press Ltd

Unit 10 Ridgewood Industrial Park,

Uckfield, East Sussex,

TN22 5QE England

Tel: +44 (0) 1825 749494

www.naval-military-press.com

www.nmarchive.com

This diary has been reprinted in facsimile from the original. Any imperfections are inevitably reproduced and the quality may fall short of modern type and cartographic standards.

Contents

LOWLAND (9th) DIVISION

3 LOWLAND BDE

1/4 BN R SCOTS FUS

1919 APR - 1919 AUG

From 52 DIV 155 BDE

Instructions regarding War Diaries and Intelligence Summaries are contained in F. S. Regs., Part II. and the Staff Manual respectively. Title pages will be prepared in manuscript.

Sheet No 1

WAR DIARY of 1/4 Bn. ~~or INTELLIGENCE SUMMARY.~~ ROYAL SCOTS FUSILIERS for APRIL 1919

(Erase heading not required.)

Army Form C. 2118.

From 52 DIV
155 BDE

Vol 13

Place	Date	Hour	Summary of Events and Information	Remarks and references to Appendices
	April			
HILDEN	1st		Routine as usual with this exception. Commanding Officers Orderly Room to be held at 1220 hours daily in future. Training. "A" & "B" Coys were struck off all duties for the month of April in order that they might carry out Section & Platoon training. Duties:- All duties to be performed by "C" & "D" Coys. "D" Coy on outpost duty. Junior officers & NCOs classes as usual. No specialist training took place on this date. The Commanding Officer attended as President of the Summary Court at HILDEN. Capt S.W. Scott attended as member of a Court of Enquiry held at RHENANIA Petroleum works at HOLTHAUSEN. Capt R. WALKINGSHAW, M.C. assumed command of letter "B" Coy vice Capt. A. Cooper M.C. as from 31/3/19. The "Cologne Post" 1st copy was sold in the canteen, price 20 Pfg. This paper to be sold daily in the Canteen in future. 2/Lieut J.H. Cunningham transferred from 1st Bn. on 10/3/19 reported for duty from U.K. leave and was posted to "B" Coy.	
"	2nd		A & B Coys carried out Section & platoon training. Junior officers & NCO classes as usual. "C" Coy carried out working on the Bde front. The G.O.C. Lowland Division visited the ~~[illegible]~~ DIEKHAUS outpost.	

(A9175) Wt W2358/P360 600,000 12/17 D. D. & L. Sch. 52a. Forms/C2118/15.

Cls.

20.B
12 sheets

Sheet 2.

Instructions regarding War Diaries and Intelligence Summaries are contained in F. S. Regs., Part II. and the Staff Manual respectively. Title pages will be prepared in manuscript.

WAR DIARY of 1/4 Bn. ROYAL SCOTS FUSILIERS.

~~INTELLIGENCE SUMMARY.~~

(Erase heading not required.)

for April 1919.

Army Form C. 2118.

Place	Date	Hour	Summary of Events and Information	Remarks and references to Appendices
	April			
HILDEN.	3.		Training as on 2nd. 'C' Coy carried out wiring on the Bde front. The Bn. was on Bde. duties. The Bde Guard was inspected by the Adjutant at 1500 hours. 2/Lt R. I. Williamson & M. S. Smith attended as members of a Summary Court which assembled at 0900 hrs at HILDEN. A notice was published in Bn. R.O warning all ranks against accepting British Bank notes in shops or restaurants in Germany. The reason for this being that BOLSHEVIST & SPARTICIST agents are known to be issuing counterfeit British Bank Notes intended for use amongst British Troops of Occupation (Ref sub order 3, 28th Inf Bde R.O. No. 103 dated 1/4/19. Summary Court. A notice was published in orders to the effect that on and after April 4th there will only be one Summary Court for the Bde Area. This will be held daily at 1000 hours (Sundays excepted) at 12 MITTEL STRASSE, BENRATH. Cinema – BENRATH. In future there will be three cinema performances weekly – Tuesday, Thursday & Friday at 1800 hours. 2/Lt E. G. L. Kidd reported from U.K. leave. The cadre of the 2nd Bn proceeded to U.K. leaving HILDEN at 0600.	
"	4th.		Training as usual. 'C' Coy carried out wiring on the Bde front. The Commanding Officer attended the Summary Court at BENRATH as President of the Court. Lieut (A/Capt) J. J. Campbell, Lieut (A/Capt) W. McIndoe reported for duty from 12th R. Sc. Fus. 2/Lt F. S. Blanckenberg reported from 2nd Army College. Capt & Qmr J. F. Anderson reported for duty and took over duties of Qmr. from 2/Lt R. Watt.	

Ch.

Sheet 3.

Instructions regarding War Diaries and Intelligence Summaries are contained in F. S. Regs., Part II. and the Staff Manual respectively. Title pages will be prepared in manuscript.

WAR DIARY or ~~INTELLIGENCE SUMMARY.~~ of 1/4 Bn. ROYAL SCOTS FUSILIERS. for April 1919

(Erase heading not required.)

Army Form C. 2118.

Place	Date	Hour	Summary of Events and Information	Remarks and references to Appendices
HILDEN.	April 5th		The Commanding Officer inspected the billets of 'A' & 'B' Coys starting at 0930. The 2nd Command inspected the billets of 'C' & 'D' Coys starting at 0930. Commanding Officer inspected all limbers and cookers and the Lewis Gun officer inspected all Lewis guns. The M.O. inspected A B C & Hq. coys after the C.O's inspections. A notice was published in Bn R.Os. warning all ranks that on no account can Civilians be shot, arrested or interfered with when in the Neutral Zone without reference to Bde Hqrs. Lieut A. J. Corrigan Lovat Scouts, attd. 1/4 R Sc Fus. assumed duties of Bde. Education Officer on 4/4/19. A/Lieut R. Watt left the Bn. for demobilization on this date. 2/Lieut G. L. Lack MC was appointed Bn. Scout Officer vice 2/Lt J. B. McMurtrie M.C., who proceeded to U.K. for demobilization.	
"	6th		Church parades were held as follows. Roman Catholics at 0845 in Catholic Church, HILDEN. Presbyterians at 1030 in the REALSCHULE. C of E. at 1120 in Church Army Institute, HILDEN. After Church parade Lieut HALLAM gave a lecture to the Bn. on recruiting for the Post Bellum Army. The Bn was on Bde duties. The Bde Guard was inspected by the Adjt at 1500 hours. Lieut (A/Capt) J. Courtenay, 2/Lts H. McKelvie & G. Galbraith left Bn for demobilisation.	
"	7th		'A' & 'B' Coys carried out close order drill. 'C' Coy carried out wiring on the Bde front. 'C, D', Hq. Coys & Transport were bathed & supplied with clean clothing.	

Ctd.

(A9573) W.W. 3357/P.90 600,000 12/17 D.D.&L. Sch. 52a. Forms/C2118/13.

Sheet 4

Instructions regarding War Diaries and Intelligence Summaries are contained in F. S. Regs., Part II. and the Staff Manual respectively. Title pages will be prepared in manuscript.

WAR DIARY ~~or INTELLIGENCE SUMMARY.~~ of 1/4 Bn. ROYAL SCOTS FUSILIERS for April 1919

(Erase heading not required.)

Army Form C. 2118.

Place	Date	Hour	Summary of Events and Information	Remarks and references to Appendices
HILDEN	April 7th		Major J.A. McEwen & Capt. A Gibson M.C. attended as President & member respectively a F.G.C.M. assembling at Hqrs 1/8 Scottish Rifles, HILDEN at 1000 hours. Capt. W.C. Stevenson attended as a member a Court of Inquiry assembling at BENRATH at 1000 hours	
"	8th		Routine as usual. Training coys carried out Section & Platoon training. Junior Officers & NCOs classes as usual. 'C' Coy carried out wiring on the Bde front. There was no specialist training on this date. The Bn Quarter Guard was inspected by the 2nd command on mounting. This to be done daily as well as the Bde Hq. Guard when furnished by the Bn. The BGC visited the training coys and the ~~ME IDE~~ ~~EICHER~~ DIEKHAUS & KEMPERDICK WE. outposts today. Lieut W McIndoe was posted to 'D' Coy & 2/Lt F. T. Blanckenberg to 'A' Coy. 2/Lt J. Reid took over the duties of Signalling Officer from Lieut J. Dalziel who rejoined 'B' Coy. The Commanding Officer attended as President of the Summary Court at BENRATH today. 'A' & 'B' Coys were bathed & supplied with clean clothing.	
"	9th		Routine & training as on previous days of month. 'C' Coy furnished a wiring party for the Bde front. 'C' Coy relieved 'D' Coy at the ~~ME IDE~~ ~~EICHER~~ DIEKHAUS to KEMPERDICK outposts. The Bn was on Bde duties. The Bde Hq Guard was inspected by the 2nd in command at 1500 hours. Starting from today there will be a Bn Field Officer of the day. He has to visit all Guards of the Bn once by day & once by night. Lieut J. J. Campbell was posted to 'C' Coy. 2/Lieut A.C. Bunting took up duties today as [illegible] Divl Hq. [illegible]	

Army Form C. 2118.

Sheet 5.

Instructions regarding War Diaries and Intelligence Summaries are contained in F. S. Regs., Part II. and the Staff Manual respectively. Title pages will be prepared in manuscript.

WAR DIARY
or
~~INTELLIGENCE SUMMARY.~~
(Erase heading not required.)

1/4th R. ROYAL SCOTS FUSILIERS for April 1919.

Place	Date	Hour	Summary of Events and Information	Remarks and references to Appendices
	April			
HILDEN	9th	[illegible]	as Divl. Educat Offr. A lecture for all students attending Bde education classes was given in the Lecture Hall, REALSCHULE today at 1045 hours.	
"	10th		Routine as usual. ~~W~~ B Coy carried out platoon & section training. 'A' Coy carried out firing practice on the Brigade range at URDENBACH - practice consisted of 5 rounds per man application at 200 yards. Men waiting to fire carried out training behind the firing point. Lieut. W. McIndoe M.C. took over command of 'D' Coy from Lieut (A/Capt) J.W. Scott as from this date. Lieut J. Dalziel took over command of 'B' Coy from Lieut (A/Capt) R. Walkingshaw M.C. as from this date. Lieut J. W. Scott proceeded to UK for demobilization.	
"	11th		Routine as usual. A & B Coys carried out Section & Platoon training. 'D' Coy carried out wiring on the Bde front. Junior Officers & NCOs classes as usual. The Commanding Officer attended as President, Summary Court at BENRATH. 2/Lt. A. P. Main reported for duty from 12th Bn R Sc Fus. He was posted to this Unit on 4.4.19. Lieut (A/Capt) R. Walkingshaw proceeded to U.K. for demobilisation.	
"	12th		The Commanding Officer inspected the billets of "A" & "B" Coys starting at 0930 hours and limbers & cookers of all Coys. The 2 i/c command inspected the billets of 'C' & 'D' Coys. The Lewis Gun Officer inspected all Coy Lewis Guns. After the billet inspection, the M.O. inspected all the men of the Bn	

Cto.

Sheet 6.

Instructions regarding War Diaries and Intelligence Summaries are contained in F. S. Regs., Part II. and the Staff Manual respectively. Title pages will be prepared in manuscript.

WAR DIARY ~~or INTELLIGENCE SUMMARY.~~ of 1/4th Bn ROYAL SCOTS FUSILIERS. for April 1919.

(Erase heading not required.)

Army Form C. 2118.

Place	Date	Hour	Summary of Events and Information	Remarks and references to Appendices
HILDEN	April 12th	contd.	The Bn was on Bde duties on this date. The Bde Hqrs Guard was inspected by the 2 i/c command at 1500 hours. It was notified in Bn orders that in future the outposts will be visited once every day by the O.C. Coy or the 2 i/c command of the Coy furnishing the outposts. O.C. Coys were instructed to explain all practices in the General Musketry Course to all ranks under their command and to practise muscle exercises on each musketry parade as well as rapid firing as frequently as possible. The following are the only examining posts in the Bde Area and all traffic passing to or from the Neutral Zone must pass through these; ~~otherwise~~ any person using another road will be charged with attempting to evade examination — HIMMELGEISTAR ~~HIMMELGIEST~~, HOLTHAUSEN, ZEUGLAGER, REIS, DIEKHAUS, KEMPERDICK. At 12.00 hours on the night of 11th - 12th owing to the conflict in DUSSELDORF between Govt. troops and Spartacists the following action was taken on orders from 3rd Low. Bde Hqrs. 1. One platoon per Coy was detailed as inlying picquet to remain under arms. 2. Parties were held in readiness to reinforce examining guards 3. Single sentries were doubled 4 Troops remained in vicinity of quarters till the warning was cancelled 5. Two sections were held in readiness to proceed to Guard the RATHAUS, HILDEN and two sections to guard the POST OFFICE, HILDEN. 6. All officers were ordered to carry	

Cto.

Sheet 4.

Instructions regarding War Diaries and Intelligence Summaries are contained in F. S. Regs., Part II. and the Staff Manual respectively. Title pages will be prepared in manuscript.

WAR DIARY of 1/4th ROYAL SCOTS FUSILIERS
~~or INTELLIGENCE SUMMARY.~~
(Erase heading not required.)

for April 1919

Army Form C. 2118.

Place	Date	Hour	Summary of Events and Information	Remarks and references to Appendices
HILDEN	April 12th	Contd.	revolvers. No further action was taken and with the exception of No. 6 all orders were cancelled on instructions from Bde Hqrs at 1305 hours. 2/Lt J. Harrison, Border Regt attd 1/4 RSF has reported to Div. Hq today as a staff learner. 2/Lt A.P. Mann was posted to "D" Coy on this date.	
"	13th		Following church parades took place. Roman Catholics at 0900 hours in Catholic Church, HILDEN, Presbyterian at 1015 hours in the REALSCHULE, HILDEN, Church of England at 1130 in Church Army Institute, HILDEN. Holy Communion for C of E was held at 0830 & 1130. There was a Company Commanders conference on this date.	
"	14th		Routine was as usual. "A" Coy carried out platoon & section training whilst "B" Coy was on the range at URDENBACH. The practice consisted of 5 rounds grouping at 100 yds. Men waiting to fire were instructed in judging distance and visual training. The Scout Officer verified ranges with the Barr & Stroud Rangefinder. A tea meal was supplied at the range. "C", "D" & Hq Coy & transport were bathed & received a change of clothing. A lecture on "Venereal Disease" was delivered by the Rev. G.L. Heaslett, B.A. in the REALSCHULE, HILDEN at 1430 hours. All officers not on duty and 20 men per coy attended. It was notified in Bn Orders that under no circumstances whatever will any officer, WO, NCO or man or vehicle proceed into the Neutral Zone without a permit signed by the Bde. Commander.	

Clo.

Instructions regarding War Diaries and Intelligence Summaries are contained in F. S. Regs., Part II. and the Staff Manual respectively. Title pages will be prepared in manuscript.

Sheet 8.

WAR DIARY of 1/4 Bn ROYAL SCOTS FUSILIERS for April 1919.

~~INTELLIGENCE SUMMARY.~~

(Erase heading not required.)

Army Form C. 2118.

Place	Date	Hour	Summary of Events and Information	Remarks and references to Appendices
HILDEN	April 15th		Routine as usual, training Coys carried out Section & Platoon training with exception that retreat was at 1430 hours. Specialist training, P.T., Junior Officers & NCOs classes were held as before. 'D' Coy carried out wiring on the Bde. front. The Bn was on Bde duties & the Bde Gd. was inspected by the 2 i/c Command at 1500 hrs. 'A' & 'B' Coys were bathed & each man supplied with clean clothing. A lecture was delivered in the REALSCHULE by Mr Y. E. Wing on "How the Navy helped the Army to win the War". This lecture was illustrated by lantern slides. From this date the Army of Occupation will be known as "The British Army of the Rhine". Lieut J.J. Campbell assumed command of C Coy vice Lieut (A/Capt) A. Gibson MC.	
"	16th		Routine & training as on previous day. Guard mounting took place at retreat, this to be the rule in future. The Commanding Officer attended the Summary Court at BENRATH as President. 2/Lt Northwood proceeded to U.K. for demobilization.	
"	14th		'B' Coy carried out Section & Platoon training. 'A' Coy was on the range. Practice consisted of 5 rounds grouping at 100 yds. 'D' Coy carried out wiring on the Bde. front. The Bn was on Bde. duties & the Bde Hq. Guard was inspected by the 2 i/c Command at 1500 hours. The Bde Gas NCO inspected all Gas respirators. 'D' Coy relieved 'C' Coy on the outposts. A German class for Officers was started today, this class to be held on Mondays & Thursdays till further notice. Lieut A. Gibson MC & 2/Lt T. Robertson proceeded to U.K. for demobilisation. 2/Lts W.W.C. Fulton & D Marshall proceeded to join the 12th Bn R.S. Fus.	

Clo.

(A9375) Wt W 3300/P500 650,000 12/17 D. D. & L. Sch. 52a. Forms/C2118/15.

Sheet 9.

Instructions regarding War Diaries and Intelligence Summaries are contained in F. S. Regs., Part II. and the Staff Manual respectively. Title pages will be prepared in manuscript.

WAR DIARY or ~~INTELLIGENCE SUMMARY.~~

(Erase heading not required.)

~~1/4 Bn~~ 1/4 ROYAL SCOTS FUSILIERS for April 1919

Army Form C. 2118.

Place	Date	Hour	Summary of Events and Information	Remarks and references to Appendices
HILDEN	April 18th		This day being Good Friday was observed as a holiday. Church parades were held ~~for~~ Roman Catholics, Presbyterians & C of E. The Divl. Commander inspected the outpost line today.	
"	19th		The usual weekly billet inspections were carried out by Coy commanders and Lewis Guns by the Lewis Gun Officer. The M.O. inspected the men after the billet inspection. The last period of the forenoon was devoted to P.T. and specialist training. The Bn was on Bde duties. Major J.A. McEwan & Lieut J. L. R. Earle-White attended a G.C.M. at BENRATH as witness & prosecutor respectively. Genl. Sir Wm Robertson, C in C, visited the HILDEN area in the afternoon.	
"	20th		Routine as usual. Church parades were held for R.Cs, Presbyterians and C of E. T/Capt J. Murray MC, Lieut H.S. Nixon, 2/Lt. W.L. Kenning & 2/Lt R.A. Guild reported from 10th H.L.I for duty.	
"	21st		Easter Monday. This was a holiday. Capt. J. G. Lochhead MC, Lieut J. K. Murray MC, Lieut W. Smellie MC & 2/Lt J. Breleny all of the R.S. Fus. reported for duty from the 15th H.L.I. The following officers ~~reported~~ all of the R.S.F. Fus. reported for duty from the 57th H.L.I. - Capt. J. Gibson Graham M.C., Lieut G.A. Foote, Lieut R. Barclay, 2/Lt F. Stoddart, 2/Lt C. J. Austin & 2/Lt H. Hamilton MM. Capt J. Murray M.C. took over command of C Coy from Lieut J. L. Campbell.	

(A9475) Wt W2355/P360 600,000 12/17 D. D. & L. Sch. 52a. Forms/C2118/15.

Cb.

Sheet 10.

Instructions regarding War Diaries and Intelligence Summaries are contained in F. S. Regs., Part II. and the Staff Manual respectively. Title pages will be prepared in manuscript.

WAR DIARY of 1/4 Bn. ROYAL SCOTS FUSILIERS.

~~or INTELLIGENCE SUMMARY.~~

(Erase heading not required.)

for April 1919.

Army Form C. 2118.

Place	Date	Hour	Summary of Events and Information	Remarks and references to Appendices
HILDEN	April 22nd.		Retreat was changed to 1800 hours - other routine was as before. Training Coys carried out Section & platoon training. Junior Officers & NCOs classes as usual. ~~[illegible]~~ The A & B Coys were bathed & received a change of clothing. An examining Board composed of Capt W.C. Stevenson R.S. Fus, 2/Lt A.M. Backie R.S. Fus. & Capt Cathcart RAVC assembled at the transport lines to examine shoeing smiths. The Commanding Officer attended as President Summary Court at BENRATH. Lieut G. Robertson attended as a member, a F.G.C.M. at Hqrs, 9th Sco. Rifles, BENRATH. Capt J. G. Graham MC took over command of 'B' Coy from Lieut J Dalziel and Capt J. G Lochhead M.C. took over command of 'D' Coy from Lieut W. McIndoe MC. Boxing & gymnasium classes were started on this date, these classes to be continued daily so long as training is being carried out.	
"	23rd.		Routine and training as on previous day. The Bn was on Bde duties & the Bde Hq Guard was inspected by the G. O. C. commanding at 1415 hours. A Coy Commanders conference was held on this date. The Bn. football team ~~[illegible]~~ played the 5/6th R. Scots in the first round of the Bde competitions to select the team to represent the Lowland Division against the N.Z.A. Army team. The result was a draw.	
"	24th.		Whilst 'B' Coy repeated its previous practice on the range, 'A' Coy carried out Section & Platoon training. Lieut W Murchie M.C & 15 O.R. proceeded to 3rd Lowland Bde L.T.M. Bty.	

(A9175) Wt W2358/P360 600,000 12/17 D. D. & L. Sch. 52a. Forms/C2118/15.

CA.

Instructions regarding War Diaries and Intelligence Summaries are contained in F. S. Regs., Part II. and the Staff Manual respectively. Title pages will be prepared in manuscript.

Sheet 11.

WAR DIARY ~~or INTELLIGENCE SUMMARY~~ of 1/4 Bn. ROYAL SCOTS FUSILIERS. for April 1919.

(Erase heading not required.)

Army Form C. 2118.

Place	Date	Hour	Summary of Events and Information	Remarks and references to Appendices
HILDEN.	April 25th		Routine as usual. Training took the form of rapid wiring on the Bde. front. "C" & "D" Coys were bathed & received ~~a change of~~ clean clothing. The Bn was on Bde duties & the Bde Hq. Guard was inspected by the 2nd i/c Command at 1415 Hours. 2/Lieut. H.M. Findlay, R.Sc.Fus. reported for duty from the 5th H.L.I.	
"	26th		Lights out was changed on this date to 2145 hours, roll call to 2115 & Staff Parade to 2130. Other routine as usual. The 2 i/c Command inspected the Billets, cookers & limbers of the Bn, whilst the Lewis Gun Officer inspected all Coy Lewis guns and the Medical Officer carried out his usual weekly inspection. The Commanding Officer attended, as President, Summary Court at BENRATH. The Bn team beat the 5/6 R. Scots team by 3 goals to 0 in the Div. competition.	
"	27th		The following change in routine took place – Roll call 2130, Staff Parade 2145, Lights Out 2200 hrs. R.Cs, Presbyterians & C of E. attended church parades. The Bn was on Bde duties & the Bde Hq. Guard was inspected by the 2 i/c Command at 1415 hours.	
"	28th		Routine as on 27th. An inter-company competition was held on the Bde. range at URDENBACH. A, B, HQ Coy & Transport were bathed and received clean clothing. Capt M. Gilmour, R.Sc.Fus. reported for duty from 9th Sco. Rifles.	
"	29th		Routine as usual. Training Coys carried out platoon & section training. "C" & "D" Coys were bathed & received clean clothing. The Bn was on duty & the Bde Hq. Guard was	

(B9175) Wt. W5369/M1293 750,000 1/17 D.D.&L. Sch. 52a. Forms/C2118/15.

C.G.

Sheet 12,

Instructions regarding War Diaries and Intelligence Summaries are contained in F. S. Regs., Part II. and the Staff Manual respectively. Title pages will be prepared in manuscript.

WAR DIARY of 1/4 Bn ROYAL SCOTS FUSILIERS for April 1919.

~~or INTELLIGENCE SUMMARY.~~

(Erase heading not required.)

Army Form C. 2118.

Place	Date	Hour	Summary of Events and Information	Remarks and references to Appendices
HILDEN	April 29th	Contd.	inspected by the Area Commandant 1415 hours. A G.C.M. was held in the REALSCHULE, HILDEN. Major J.A. McEwen attended as Prosecutor & Capt J. G. Graham M.C. as member.	
"	30th		Routine as usual. 'A' Coy completed its month's Section & Platoon training. 'B' Coy carried out rapid wiring on the Bde front. P.T. & specialist training as usual. 'A' Coy relieved 'C' Coy on the ~~HEIDE, EICHERT~~ DIEKHAUS, KEMPERDICK & REISHOLZ outposts. The Bn provided a Guard for Divl. Hqrs. This guard was inspected by the Adjutant. The G.C.M. which assembled on the previous day was continued on this date. The Commanding Officer attended, as President, Summary Court at BENRATH. Instead of there being a Field Officer of the day, a Field Officer of the Week will be appointed. He must visit all guards once by day and once by night at least three times during his tour of duty. The Bn football team beat the 15th H.L.I. in the final of the Divl competition by 3 goals to 2 and was chosen to represent the Lowland Divn against the U.S.A. Army team.	

[illegible] Lt Col.
Cdg 1/4 R. Scots Fusiliers

(A9175) Wt W2353/P560 600,000 12/17 D. D. & L. Sch. 52a. Forms/C2118/15.

Instructions regarding War Diaries and Intelligence Summaries are contained in F. S. Regs., Part II. and the Staff Manual respectively. Title pages will be prepared in manuscript.

WAR DIARY
or
INTELLIGENCE SUMMARY.
(Erase heading not required.)

1/4th Battalion Royal Scots Fusiliers

Army Form C. 2118.

Place	Date	Hour	Summary of Events and Information	Remarks and references to Appendices
HILDEN	May 1st		"C" & "D" Companies became Training Companies, A & B Companies became duty Companies. Section & Platoon training carried out by C & D Coys. A Coy furnished pickets. C Coy carried out [illegible] on the left sub sector of the Brigade front. [illegible] of A, B, H.Q. Coys [illegible] [illegible] D.R.O. [illegible] [illegible] 2100 hours nightly. B.R.O. 1668. All W.O's, N.C.O's & O.R's [illegible] 2201 [illegible]	
	2nd		"D" Coy carried out Section & Platoon training. [illegible] musketry [illegible]. LECTURE. A Lecture on [illegible] was given [illegible] at 1730 hrs in the [illegible] HILDEN, 2 Officers & 150 O.R's [illegible]. Audit Board. An Audit Board [illegible] the following [illegible] 1) Officers Mess funds, 2) [illegible] Mess funds, 3) P.R.I. funds, 4) Sports fund, 5) [illegible] President – Major [illegible] Members – Lt. [illegible] The Battn Football Team [illegible] ANDERNACH [illegible]	
	3rd		Usual Commanding Officer's Billet inspection & [illegible] for [illegible] Competition was carried out. The M.O. held his weekly Medical Inspection. [illegible] Courses. 2/Lt H. McFindlay proceeded to MONTJOIE for a Course at Army [illegible] School. [illegible] ANDERNACH [illegible] Result of football match 4th R.S.F. 7 goals 36th American [illegible] Audit Board. 2/Lt [illegible] detailed as member [illegible]	
	4th		Church Parades as usual. The following Officers were transferred to 11th R.S.F. at DINKIRK [illegible] Capt. McGilmour, [illegible] D.M. Gardiner, R. Hamilton, W. [illegible] J. Lindsay, [illegible] J. McWhirter [illegible]	

D. D. & L., London, E.C. (a3140) Wt W3300/P713 750,000 3/18 E 2688 Forms/C2118/16.

U.B.
7 [illegible]

Instructions regarding War Diaries and Intelligence Summaries are contained in F. S. Regs., Part II. and the Staff Manual respectively. Title pages will be prepared in manuscript.

WAR DIARY
or
~~INTELLIGENCE SUMMARY.~~ 1/4th Battalion Royal Scots Fusiliers

(Erase heading not required.)

Army Form C. 2118.

(2)

Place	Date	Hour	Summary of Events and Information	Remarks and references to Appendices
HILDEN	May 4th		continued. The following officers were transferred to 5/6 [illegible] on this date under [illegible] S.C. 104 of 2/5/19: — Lt. A.E. [illegible], 2/Lt. [illegible], S.E.S. [illegible], J.S. [illegible], [illegible]. 2/Lt. A.A. [illegible] should have proceeded with above [illegible]. Lt. H. J. [illegible] [illegible]. 2/Lt. [illegible] Kidd & 2/Lt. J. McWhirter.	
	5th		Routine as usual. C Coy. [illegible] Section & Platoon Training. D Coy. [illegible] on Rifle Range. Baths [illegible]. Baths — B, C, H.Q. Coys & Transport were allotted Baths on this date. Result of football match: 4th R.S.F. 6 goals, 10th AMERICAN FIELD ARTILLERY 2 goals.	
	6th		Routine as usual. D Coy. carried out training. C Coy. [illegible]. Baths were allotted to A & D Coys. [illegible] B Coy. relieved A Coy. [illegible] Nos. 1, 2 – 4.	
	7th		There was no training on this date owing to [illegible] Bde. [illegible]. D Coy. [illegible]. 2nd in Command [illegible] HILDEN [illegible]. Church Parade. [illegible] HILDEN – HAAN [illegible]. 2nd Lt. A.T. [illegible] [illegible] 1720 [illegible]. [illegible]	
	8th		D Coy. carried out Section & Platoon Training. [illegible] A & B Coys. [illegible] Bde. [illegible]. Published for information in Bn. R.O. that [illegible] will be substituted 1/4th R.S. Fus. [illegible]	

(4)

D. D. & L., London, E.C. (20340) Wt W5300/P713 750,000 3/18 E 2688 Forms/C2118/16.

Instructions regarding War Diaries and Intelligence Summaries are contained in F. S. Regs., Part II. and the Staff Manual respectively. Title pages will be prepared in manuscript.

Army Form C. 2118.

WAR DIARY
or
INTELLIGENCE SUMMARY.
(Erase heading not required.)

1/4th Battalion Royal Scots Fusiliers. (3)

Place	Date	Hour	Summary of Events and Information	Remarks and references to Appendices
HILDEN	May 9th		'C' & 'D' Coy's carried out Section & Platoon Training. Battn found Brigade [illegible] 'D' Coy [illegible]. 'A' & 'D' Coys [illegible] Bde [illegible]. 1st Lt G. Ramsay [illegible] att'd 1/4 R.S.F. [illegible] [illegible] HILDEN at 1720 hrs. Battn [illegible]	
	10th		Usual Commanding Officer's [illegible] Capt. G. [illegible] [illegible] from this date. [illegible] 'C' Company ordered [illegible] once a week [illegible] in [illegible] order [illegible]	
	11th		Church Parades as usual. Bn found Bde [illegible], Bde guard [illegible] by 'B' Coy.	
	12th		'C' Coy carried out Section & Platoon Training. 'D' Coy carried out [illegible] & judging distance at the Range.	
	13th		'C' Coy carried out the same training. 'D' Coy was duty Coy. [illegible] by D Coy. [illegible] 11th Corps [illegible] in the use of [illegible]. Battn found Bde [illegible] by D Coy. [illegible] in the Rhine [illegible]	
	14th		C Coy carried out [illegible] 'A' 'B' & 'D' Coys [illegible] Lt. J. M. Paul R.S.F. selected for [illegible] course at BONN [illegible] from 51st H.L.I. [illegible] 1/4th R.S.F. moved to BENRATH [illegible]	

D. D. & L., London, E.C.
(10340) Wt W5300/P713 750,000 3/18 .. 1688 Forms/C2118/16.

Instructions regarding War Diaries and Intelligence Summaries are contained in F. S. Regs., Part II. and the Staff Manual respectively. Title pages will be prepared in manuscript.

WAR DIARY or INTELLIGENCE SUMMARY.

1/4th Battalion Royal Scots Fusiliers

(Erase heading not required.)

Army Form C. 2118.

(4)

Place	Date	Hour	Summary of Events and Information	Remarks and references to Appendices
HILDEN	May 15th		Training was cancelled by BMX5 3rd Low Bde dated 14/5/19. In accordance with this message the following action was taken & report sent to Bde.	
			The Battn paraded in fighting order at 08.30 hrs under Major J. A. [illegible] strength 14 Officers 195 O.R's. [illegible] were also taken.	
			Battn marched to the following factories :- (1) [illegible] KOPPEL (2) RHEINISCHE STOHLWERKE (3) RHEINISCHE SCHIEFERMITTELWERKE (4) SCHLIEFER & LANG (5) KAMPF & SPINDLER. The [illegible] of these factories [illegible] on strike for 3 days but returned to work this morning. [illegible] the Managing Director or a Partner of each firm. The Director of RHEINISCHE STOHLWERKE stated that in his opinion most of the workmen desired to work but they were overruled by a minority of [illegible].	
			A Partner of KAMPF & SPINDLER'S stated that he understood the strikers [illegible] resumed work in accordance with orders issued by British Military Authorities but threatened to call a general strike if [illegible] of demands made by them [illegible] agreed to by their employers. The strike would include Gas, Electric Power, Water Supply etc. & would take place on the following Monday.	
			He also stated that [illegible] [illegible] 13 [illegible] in the event of Industrial [illegible] [illegible] [illegible].	
			Battn found Bde duties. Bde guard being [illegible] by B Coy.	
			Billets of "B" & "C" Coys [illegible]. HILDEN & REISHOLZ [illegible] to all Troops not [illegible] by [illegible] BRO 224 of 15/5/19.	
			Result Officers Football Match: Mr Fawcett XI 1 goal, Mr Hamilton's XI Nil.	
	16th		The Compulsory Educational Scheme was started on this date. [illegible] Military Training. All available O.R's [illegible] paraded at 08.45 hrs for the purpose of organising the Educational Classes. The scheme [illegible] Educational training for 6 hours in each week viz. 09.00 – 12.00 hrs on Tuesday's & Friday's. A B.R.O. was [illegible] stating that men on being issued with new clothing may retain their old [illegible] for fatigues etc.	

D. D. & L., London, E.C.
(14340) Wt W3300/P713 750.000 3/18 ☐ 2688 Forms/C2118/16.

Instructions regarding War Diaries and Intelligence Summaries are contained in F. S. Regs., Part II. and the Staff Manual respectively. Title pages will be prepared in manuscript.

WAR DIARY
or
INTELLIGENCE SUMMARY.
(*Erase heading not required.*)

[illegible] Battalion Royal Scots Fusiliers (5)

Army Form C. 2118.

Place	Date	Hour	Summary of Events and Information	Remarks and references to Appendices
HILDEN	MAY 17th		Usual Commanding Officer's & [illegible] Officer's [illegible]. The [illegible] guards at [illegible] & [illegible] were taken over by A Coy, B & C Coys respectively. All [illegible] of C Coy at REICHHOLZ(?) POST was relieved by A Coy. [illegible] by D Coy [illegible] at 17.15 hrs.	
	18th		Church Parades as usual. A competition was held in the afternoon [illegible] between teams of Officers, W.O.s & Serjeants, Corporals & Privates. [illegible] Result of competition as follows:—	
	19th		Routine as usual. Owing to the many duties being performed by the Battn. on this date no Coy. training was carried out with the exception of [illegible] classes. Outpost Relief. The Battn. [illegible] FRIEDHOF(?) OUTPOST. [illegible] by 1 Off. & 15 O.Rs. of B Coy. [illegible] Baths were allotted to A, B, C & HQ Coys & Transport from 13.30 hrs onwards.	
	20th		All ranks [illegible] for [illegible]. Gymnasium & Boxing Classes [illegible] until further notice. Outpost Relief. D Coy relieved B Coy at the FRIEDHOF(?) POST. [illegible] S.B.R. [illegible]	

	200x	300x	Total
Officers	114	109	223
W.O.s & Sgts	112	99	211
Privates	74	[illegible]	[illegible]
Corporals	96	81	177

Highest [illegible] by individuals:

C.S.M. Munro	32
[illegible]	31
[illegible]	[illegible]
Capt. J. [illegible]	30
[illegible]	[illegible]
2nd Lt. [illegible]	29

Tea was provided at the Range.

D. D. & L., London, E.C.
(10340) Wt W3300/P713 750,000 3/18 1658 Forms/C2118/16.

Instructions regarding War Diaries and Intelligence Summaries are contained in F. S. Regs., Part II. and the Staff Manual respectively. Title pages will be prepared in manuscript.

WAR DIARY
or
INTELLIGENCE SUMMARY.
(Erase heading not required.)

1st Battalion Royal Irish [illegible]

Army Form C. 2118.

Place	Date MAY	Hour	Summary of Events and Information	Remarks and references to Appendices
HILDEN	21st		Training carried out under Company arrangements. [illegible] B Coy. [illegible] The B.G.C. [illegible] Nos 1, 2, 3 & 4 on this date [illegible] being very satisfied with the [illegible] of the Battalion. Gen. Sir W. Robertson passed through the area.	
	22nd		Training. [illegible] all available [illegible]	
	23rd		Routine as usual. All available men of the Battn paraded at [illegible] on this date for [illegible]. A Lecture on "Shakespearean [illegible]" was given [illegible] by Mr. [illegible] at 11.00 am in the [illegible]. Battalion [illegible]	
	24th		Routine as usual. [illegible] Commanding Officer's [illegible] of [illegible] A Garden Fête took place in the [illegible] Gardens, BENRATH, organised by the 3rd [illegible] Bde.	
	25th		Routine as usual. [illegible] Garden Fête at BENRATH was continued.	
	26th		No training took place [illegible] [illegible] Battn found [illegible] Baths [illegible] A, B, C [illegible] [illegible] A Company of Tanks arrived [illegible] on this date.	
	27th		All available men paraded at [illegible] [illegible]	

D. D. & L., London, E.C.
(10340) Wt W3300/P713 750,000 3/18 C 2688 Forms/C2118/16.

Instructions regarding War Diaries and Intelligence Summaries are contained in F. S. Regs., Part II. and the Staff Manual respectively. Title pages will be prepared in manuscript.

WAR DIARY
or
INTELLIGENCE SUMMARY.
(Erase heading not required.)

[illegible] Battalion Royal [illegible] Fusiliers

Army Form C. 2118.

Place	Date	Hour	Summary of Events and Information	Remarks and references to Appendices
HILDEN	MAY 28th		Training was cancelled owing to [illegible] at BENRATH. A composite Company under Capt. T. S. Graham M.C. [illegible] Cyclists & Lewis Gun teams to BENRATH. This Company [illegible] day & night. [illegible] of HILDEN. All men left in billets [illegible] The British [illegible] JAMES [illegible] Divisional Commander [illegible] The C.O. [illegible]	
	29th		The Battn. still [illegible] training. Composite Company still at BENRATH. Battn on Bde duties, Bde Guard [illegible] Capt. J. G. [illegible] 25/5/19 [illegible] 29/5/19. [illegible] attended a [illegible] at [illegible] 1430 hrs. [illegible] 0800 – 1800 [illegible] 5 persons may congregate at one time.	
	30th		The Battn. still [illegible] training. Composite Coy still at BENRATH. [illegible] was detailed to arrest the strikers from the HILDEN district. [illegible] were [illegible] by 3rd [illegible] Bde of the [illegible] The [illegible] of [illegible] 2130 hrs. [illegible] consisted of 1 Officer, 1 N.C.O. [illegible] & 1 German Civil Police.	
	31st		The arrest of the strikers was completed by 0200 hrs, they were retained in the Reception Room of the [illegible] under guard. At 0500 hrs they were interviewed by an officer of the 3rd [illegible] Bde Staff & when they [illegible] promise to resume work were released. They were [illegible] returned [illegible] employers. Routine as usual. Unit Commanding Officers & M.O.s [illegible] carried out. Battn on Bde duties & Guard found by the Composite Coy stationed BENRATH.	Charles [illegible] Lt Col. [illegible]

D. D. & L. London, E.C. (12340) Wt W5300/P713 750,000 3/18 2688 Forms/C2118/16.

JUNE

Army Form C. 2118.

Instructions regarding War Diaries and Intelligence Summaries are contained in F. S. Regs., Part II. and the Staff Manual respectively. Title pages will be prepared in manuscript.

WAR DIARY
or
INTELLIGENCE SUMMARY.
(Erase heading not required.)

9/6 1/4th Bn. Royal Scots Fusiliers for JUNE 1919

Place	Date	Hour	Summary of Events and Information	Remarks and references to Appendices
HILDEN	1st	—	(SUNDAY) Routine as usual. Church Parades as usual. Composite Company still at BENRATH on strike duty. The Bn. ceases to stand to but all ranks are confined to the Bn. Area.	
—	2nd	—	Routine as usual. Training carried out under company arrangements. Baths allotted to companies from 13.30 onwards, in following order "B", "A", "C", HQ Coy. Transport. Lecture: An interesting lecture was given by Prof. A. J. Wilson Hart MA FRHS on "Poland Past & Present and Future" at 11.00 hrs in the Realschule. Bn. found Bde duties. Bn. Guard furnished by "D" Coy mounted at 17.15 hrs. Composite Coy still at BENRATH.	
—	3rd		Being the birthday of His Majesty the King it was observed as a holiday. There was a short ceremonial parade at 1200 consisting of 1/4th RSF, 1/5th KOSB & a detachment of Tank Corps. Composite Coy still at BENRATH. Baths were allotted to "B" Coy. The draw for the Derby Sweepstake took place at 1400 hrs, result published in Bn. R. O. A Garden Fete was given at the Schloss Garden BENRATH in the afternoon and evening. The Band of the 1st Lancers was in attendance. Sports took place in the afternoon. Refreshments were obtainable. Smoking concert at 19.30 hrs. Proclamation by the British Authorities: "In view of the fact that the workers in the HILDEN–BENRATH area have complied with the British Military Orders the restrictions placed upon Civilians are removed."	
—	4th		Routine as usual. Training carried out under company arrangements. The Blankets of the whole Bn. were disinfected. Bn. found Bde duties. Bde Guard found by "A" Coy. Composite Coy returned to the Bn. from BENRATH.	

D. D. & L., London, E.C.
(10340) Wt W5300/P713 750,000 3/18 & 1688 Forms/C2118/16.

22.B
9 sheets

2

Instructions regarding War Diaries and Intelligence Summaries are contained in F. S. Regs., Part II. and the Staff Manual respectively. Title pages will be prepared in manuscript.

WAR DIARY

or

INTELLIGENCE SUMMARY.

(Erase heading not required.)

Army Form C. 2118.

of the 1/4th Bn. Royal Scots [illegible]

JUNE 1919

Place	Date	Hour	Summary of Events and Information	Remarks and references to Appendices
HILDEN	5th		Musketry & T. D. were carried out by Coys on Bn ranges during the morning. Capt. W. A. Hook MC, takes over command of "A" Coy from Lt/Capt. W. C. Skinner with effect from today's date. 2/Lt J. A. M. Bright was appointed [illegible] Officer with effect from today, in addition to his work as Demobilization Officer.	
—	6th		Routine as usual. All ranks paraded at 08.00 for compulsory [illegible]. Major J. A. McEwen held a class from 09.15 – 12.00 on Military Subjects. Bn from Bn Duties. Bn Guard found by "B" Coy. The following congratulatory message was sent today to Bde. Gen. E. S. Girdwood. C.B. C.M.G. commanding 3rd Lowland Bde. "All ranks 1/4th R. S. F. send heartiest [illegible] congratulations on your C.M.G."	
—	7th		Routine as usual. Usual Commanding Officer's inspection of billets. [illegible] — [illegible] and [illegible]. Usual H. O's Inspection. The following wire was received from Brigadier Gen. E. S. Girdwood C.B. C.M.G. Comd. 3rd Lowland Bde. "Sc 16 6th aaa. Very many thanks to all ranks for congratulations aaa, much appreciated."	
—	8th		Usual Church Parades. Bn on Bn Duties. Bn H. Qr Guard found by "A" Coy. A shooting match took place in the afternoon on Bn Ranges between H.Qr. Officers & H.Qr. other ranks. Teams of 8. Result H. Q. Officers 230 Pts. H.Qr. O.R. 208 points.	
—	9th		(Whit Monday) today was observed as a holiday.	

D. D. & L., London, E.C.
(10340) Wt W5300/P713 750,000 3/18 & 1888 Forms/C2118/16.

3

Instructions regarding War Diaries and Intelligence Summaries are contained in F. S. Regs., Part II. and the Staff Manual respectively. Title pages will be prepared in manuscript.

WAR DIARY
or
~~INTELLIGENCE~~ SUMMARY.
(~~Erase heading not required.~~)

Army Form C. 2118.

1/4 Bn. Royal Scots Fusiliers.

JUNE 1919. Germany.

Place	Date	Hour	Summary of Events and Information	Remarks and references to Appendices
HILDEN	10th		Routine as usual. Wiring was carried out on left sub sector of the Bde Front by 'A' 'B' 'D' Coys. 'A' supplied 2 officers & 50 O.R. 'B' 2 officers 40 men. 'D' 1 officer 30 men. Baths were allotted to coys for men not employed on wiring, Bn or Bde duties. Bde Hqrs Guard found by 'C' Coy. A lecture on the return to "Pay & Mess Book" system of accounting was given at Doral College OHLIGS at 14.45 hrs. The following were detailed to attend. The Bn Imprest Holder, Coy Commdrs, Coy CQMS & Coy Clerks. COLOGNE-CALAIS leave service. An express leave train service between the above places has now started, for the benefit of officers & men of the Rhine Army. The trains are composed of British Ambulance train stock. The strictest attention is called to the utmost care to be taken with the carriages & fittings.	
—	11th		Routine as usual. Wiring on the Bde Front was continued today, detail as for yesterday. Training was carried out under company arrangements for all men not employed in wiring. Blankets of B & D Coys were disinfected. Divisional Guard was furnished by 'D' Coy, mounting at 08.30 hrs. Lt N.D. Moore to placed on the sick list as from this date. Company Command. Lieut G.A. Patterson assumes command of 'B' Coy from T/Capt J. Gilson Graham MC (for demobilisation) with effect from this date.	
—	12th		Routine as usual, wiring on the Bde Front was continued, detail of parties as follows. 'A' Coy 2 off. 40 O.R's 'B' Coy 2 off. 50 O.R. 'D' 1 off. 31 O.R. Lt G.H. Foote was in charge of the party. Training under Coy arrangements for all ranks not employed on wiring. Bn and on Bde duties. Bde Guard furnished by "A" Coy. Lt N.D. Moore was taken off the sick list as from today.	

D. D. & L., London, E.C.
(20340) Wt W5300/P713 750,000 3/18 Sch. 2688 Forms/C2118/16.

Instructions regarding War Diaries and Intelligence Summaries are contained in F. S. Regs., Part II. and the Staff Manual respectively. Title pages will be prepared in manuscript.

4

Army Form C. 2118.

~~WAR DIARY~~ (for Dist.)
or
~~INTELLIGENCE SUMMARY.~~ of the 1/4th Bn Royal Scots Fusiliers

~~(Erase heading not required.)~~

JUNE 1919.

Place	Date	Hour	Summary of Events and Information	Remarks and references to Appendices
HILDEN	13th		Compulsory education for all other ranks. Major McEwen held a class for all available officers in Military Subjects 09-15 – 12-00 hrs. 2/Lt Buchan is temporarily transferred from "B" to "D" Coy with effect from 12-6-19. At 20-00 hrs, 4 Offrs & 100 O.R.'s left Bn H.Qrs to take up positions in front of outpost line for the purpose of catching smugglers.	
—	14th		The smugglers party returned about 02-00 hrs. Total no. of smugglers captured was 40. Routine as usual. Usual Commanding Officer's & N.C.O's inspections. Bn or Bde duties. Guard found by "C" Coy. Inter Coy Transfer Officers – Lt W. McBride MC is transferred to "C" Coy with effect from this date. Lieut [illegible] Robertson is transferred to "D" Coy with effect from this date, as Second in Command of "D" Coy and assumes the duties of Coy Commander during absence of Capt J. B. Lochhead MC in hospital. A garden Fete was given in the "SCHLOSS GARDENS" BENRATH during the afternoon & evening. The band of the 17th Lancers and an American Jazz Band were in attendance. Miss Lena Ashwell's concert party gave an open air concert in the evening. Refreshments of all kinds were available.	
—	15th		Usual Church Parades. Lts W. J. Morrison, W. D. Moore, H. S. Moir and 2/Lt W. Wallace having reported for duty from HILDEN Station Control Post are now available for duty with Coys. Commands. Major J. H. McEwen assumes command of the Bn vice Lt Col Gibb to U.K. on one month's leave.	

D. D. & L., London, E.C.
(B2340) Wt W3300/P713 750,000 3/18 Sch. 52a Forms/C2118/16

Army Form C. 2118.

WAR DIARY
or
~~INTELLIGENCE~~ SUMMARY. of the 1/4th Bn Royal Scots Fusiliers

(Erase heading not required.)

5

JUNE. 1919

Place	Date	Hour	Summary of Events and Information	Remarks and references to Appendices
HILDEN	16th		Routine as usual. The Battn. carried out Barbe-wiring on the Bde left sub-sector front. Party's were supplied by the Companies as follows: 'A' Coy. 2 Officer's 40 Men; 'B' Coy. 2 Officer's 50 Men, 'C' Coy. 1 Officer 15 Men, 'D' Coy. 1 Officer 15 Men. Training was carried out under Coy. arrangements for all men not employed in wiring. Baths were allotted to all Coy's during the afternoon. Battn. on Brigade duties — Bde. Guard furnished by 'B' Coy.	
	17th		Routine as usual. Continuing Education for all O.R's. A Lecture was given by Mr EMERSON BROWN U.S. on "The United task of the English speaking peoples" in the Realschule at 11.00 hrs. Baths were allotted to the details of all Coy's during the afternoon. Sick List. 2Lt H.M. FINDLAY is placed on the Sick List as from 14/6/19. COMMAND. Major Gen. H.H. TUDOR CB CMG assumes command of the Lowland Division vice Major Gen. Sir R.H.N. BUTLER KCB KCMG (auth. D.R.O. 497 dated 14-6-19)	
	18th		Routine as usual. Training under Coy. arrangements. Battn. on Bde. duties — Bde Guard furnished by 'D' Coy. Blankets of the Bn. were disinfected. J - 3 Day. First preparations for the advance in the event of the German failing to sign the "Peace Terms". The 3rd Highland Bde arrived during the evening. The 4th Seaforth Hdrs proceeded to OHLIGS. The 8th Black Watch proceeded to BENRATH. The 6th Black Watch were billeted in HILDEN.	

D. D. & L., London, E.C. (10340) Wt W5300/P713 750,000 3/18 1688 Forms/C2118/16.

Instructions regarding War Diaries and Intelligence Summaries are contained in F. S. Regs., Part II. and the Staff Manual respectively. Title pages will be prepared in manuscript.

WAR DIARY
or
INTELLIGENCE SUMMARY. of the 1/4th Bn Royal Scots Fusiliers

6

Army Form C. 2118.

(Erase heading not required.)

JUNE 1919.

Place	Date	Hour	Summary of Events and Information	Remarks and references to Appendices
HILDEN	19th		Routine as usual. Training under Coy. arrangements. Commanding Officers conference at Bde. H.Q. at 17.30 hrs. J – 2 Day. Further preparations made for the advance. All Outposts were relieved this day by the 6th Bn. Black Watch. A Section of the 9th Machine Gun Battn is attached to this Unit.	
	20th		Routine as usual with the exception of Sick Parade at 06.30 hrs. Training :– The whole Battn paraded on the Bn. Parade Ground at 10.30 hrs as for the move. Drawn fighting order, steel helmets slung under the right shoulder strap. The Transport was formed up in rear of the Battn. A Special Address was given by The Rev. J. R. P. SCLATER DD. of the "New North United Free Church" EDINBURGH, on the Parade ground at 11.30 hrs. Battn. on Bde duties :— Bde Guard furnished by A Coy. J – 2 Day continued owing to time extension being granted for the signing of the "Peace Terms".	
	21st		Routine as usual. Usual Commanding Officer's & Medical Officer's inspections carried out. J – 2 Day continued.	
	22nd		Routine as usual. Church Parades as usual. Special Parade for D Coy at 12.00 hrs in [illegible]. The C.O. addressed all ranks of the Coy. Lt. Col. C. GIBB having been recalled from U.K. leave resumes command of the Battn vice Major F.A. McEWEN, on 20/6/19.	

Instructions regarding War Diaries and Intelligence Summaries are contained in F. S. Regs., Part II. and the Staff Manual respectively. Title pages will be prepared in manuscript.

Army Form C. 2118.

WAR DIARY
or
INTELLIGENCE SUMMARY. of the 1/4th Bn. Royal [illegible]

(Erase heading not required.)

4

JUNE 1919.

Place	Date	Hour	Summary of Events and Information	Remarks and references to Appendices
HILDEN	22nd		continued. Bn. on Bde. duties :- Bde. guard furnished by 'C' Coy. J – 1 Day. Final preparations for the advance.	
	23rd		Routine as usual. Baths allotted to all Coy's during the day. Training carried out by Companies under Coy arrangements when not bathing. 'J' Day. Movement Orders issued. Battalion ready to move forward if Peace Terms are not signed. Decision due by 1900 hrs. Notification received from 3rd Low. Bde. H.Q.R's at 22 00 hrs that orders for the move were suspended. The German Delegates issued their intention of signing the Terms & the actual signing would take place within the next few days.	
	24th		Routine as usual. Compulsory Education for all O.R's with the exception of those recently returned from Outpost. Lecture :- A Lecture was given by Mr. F.H.M. BRIGHT to the whole Battn in the Realschule at 0900 hrs – Subject "The History of the Regiment". Training was carried out by all men recently returned from Outpost under Coy. arrangements. Battn on Bde. duties :- Bde. Guard furnished by B Coy.	

D. D. & L., London, E.C.
(20340) Wt W5300/P713 750.000 3/18 & 2688 Forms/C2118/16.

Instructions regarding War Diaries and Intelligence Summaries are contained in F. S. Regs., Part II. and the Staff Manual respectively. Title pages will be prepared in manuscript.

WAR DIARY
or
INTELLIGENCE SUMMARY. of the 1/4th Bn. Royal Scots Fusiliers [illegible]

(Erase heading not required.)

8

Army Form C. 2118.

JUNE 1919

Place	Date	Hour	Summary of Events and Information	Remarks and references to Appendices
HILDEN	25th		Routine as usual. Sick Parade at 08.00 hrs.	
			Training :- The Battn. [illegible] march at 09.15 hrs.	
			Orders received from 2nd [illegible] Bde. informing Battalions that on receipt of	
			order of day, [illegible] Bde. [illegible] make arrangements to take	
			outposts which had been handed over to the Highland Division	
			[illegible] Battns.	
	26th		Routine as usual.	
			Training :- 09.00 hrs. Adjutant's Parade for the entire Battn.	
			10.30 – 11.00. The Commanding Officer addressed the Battn. in the	
			Lecture Hall [illegible], Subject :- Esprit de Corps & Discipline, he also	
			expressed his appreciation for the Battalion's past [illegible] – [illegible]	
			[illegible] it to be [illegible] [illegible] improved.	
			Battn. on Bde. duties – Bde. Guard furnished by D Coy.	
	27th		Routine as usual.	
			A Parade was ordered at 07.30 hrs for all Ranks for the [illegible] [illegible]	
			of reading out Battn. Routine Orders.	
			Usual Educational Classes held.	
			Training was carried out by all Ranks not undergoing Education.	
			Sick List. 2Lt. G. L. JACK M.C. was placed on the Sick List as from 27-6-19.	
			The following Officers were placed on the Sick List as from this date.	
			Lt. J. DALZIEL, Lt. A. ROBERTSON, 2/Lt. A. R. MAIN.	
			Carrying of Revolvers.	
			Ref. G.R.O. 1939 dated 12th April 1919. The carrying of Revolvers by Officers	
			within the II Corps area [illegible] now be discontinued.	
			Auth. D.R.O. 235 dated 26-6-1919.	

D. D. & L., London, E.C.
(a8340) Wt W5300/P713 750,000 3/18 Z 2688 Forms/C2118/16.

Instructions regarding War Diaries and Intelligence Summaries are contained in F. S. Regs., Part II. and the Staff Manual respectively. Title pages will be prepared in manuscript.

9

Army Form C. 2118.

WAR DIARY
or
~~INTELLIGENCE SUMMARY.~~ of the 1/4th Bn. Royal Scots Fusiliers

(*Erase heading not required.*)

JUNE 1919.

Place	Date	Hour	Summary of Events and Information	Remarks and references to Appendices
HILDEN	28th		Routine as usual. Major J. A. McEWEN assumed command of the Battn. from this date vice Lt. Col. C. GIBB to U.K. on one month's special leave. The Official Photographer visited the Battn. & took photographs of all Coys. Sick List. 2 Lt. G.L. JACK M.C. is taken off the sick list as from this date. The Medical Officer carried out the usual weekly inspection. Battn. on Bde. duties — Bde. guard furnished by "A" Coy. Result of Company Football Knock-out Competition: A Coy. 7 goals. D Coy. NIL. B Coy. 3 goals. C Coy. NIL. A Wire was received from 3rd Lan. Bdes H.Q. at 15.30 the following "PEACE IS SIGNED".	
	29th		Routine as usual. Church Parades as usual. Final of Company Football Knock-out Competition took place in the evening A Coy v B Coy & resulted in a win for B Coy by 1 goal to NIL.	
	30th		Routine as usual. Training:- "A" Coy. carried out Musketry on the Rifle Range. "B" "C" & "D" Coys. paraded for Adjutant's parade on the Battn. Parade Ground at 09.15 hrs. Remainder of the morning training was carried out under Coy. arrangements. Bn. on Bde. duties — Bde. guard furnished by "C" Coy. The Battn. took over the Outposts during the afternoon relieving the 6th Bn. Black Watch Highland Division.	

J. A. McEwen
Major Commanding 1/4th R. Scots Fus.

HILDEN. 30-6-19.

D. D. & L., London, E.C.
(10540) Wt W5300/P713 750,000 3/18 Sch. 2688 Forms/C2118/16.

I

Instructions regarding War Diaries and Intelligence Summaries are contained in F. S. Regs., Part II. and the Staff Manual respectively. Title pages will be prepared in manuscript.

WAR DIARY
or
~~INTELLIGENCE~~ SUMMARY. of 1/4th Bn Royal Scots [illegible]

(Erase heading not required.)

FOR MONTH OF JULY 1919

Army Form C. 2118.

Place	Date	Hour	Summary of Events and Information	Remarks and references to Appendices
Hilden	1st		Routine as usual. Educational Parades. All other ranks, less outpost personnel and party detailed for Rhine Trip paraded under the Orderly Officer at 08.00 hrs and were taken over as usual by the Education Staff. Training under Coy arrangements was carried out by those not attending classes. 2/Lt J. P. Campbell and [illegible] reported for duty from Courses.	
do	2nd		Training under Coy arrangements and routine. Bn found Bde duties. Bde Qr Guard found by 'B' Coy. Outposts. The instructions regarding outposts remain the same as before the signing of Peace except that there will be no firing at smugglers. Transfer. 2/Lt H.A. Yates proceeded to join 3rd Lowland Bn T.M.B. for duty. Reveille, until further orders will be at 06.30 hrs.	
do.	3rd		Routine. Training. 'B' Coy less Kempen? outpost Personnel, carried out musketry on the Bde Ranges. 'A' 'C' & 'D' Coys carried out Training under the arrangements made by OC Coys. The A.D.V.S inspected the Transport and expressed himself as satisfied with turnout. B.G.C. 3rd Lowland Bde visited outposts Nos 1, 2, 3, 4, 5 this morning.	
do	4th		Declared a General Holiday. Sports were held as follows:- Cross Country run (teams of 15 per Coy), won by 'C' Coy time 14½ minutes. Result C. D. A. B. In the afternoon five a-side football took place. Results 'A' v 'D' result win for 'A'. 'B' v 'C' result win for 'B'. Final 'B' v 'A' result 'B' 1 goal v 'A' nil. A telephone message was received from 3rd Lowland Bde "Prepare to move on Monday 7th Inst by rail."	
do	5th		Routine. M.O.'s weekly inspection. Warning Order sent out to Coys re move. Capt J. Murray MC proceeded to Bensberg? to reconnoitre new area to be taken over by Bn. A garden fete at Schloss BENRATH.	[illegible]

D. D. & L., London, E.C. (10340) Wt W5,300/P718 750,000 3/18 Sch. 26a Forms/C2118/15.

Instructions regarding War Diaries and Intelligence Summaries are contained in F. S. Regs., Part II. and the Staff Manual respectively. Title pages will be prepared in manuscript.

WAR DIARY
or
~~INTELLIGENCE~~ SUMMARY.
(Erase heading not required.)

II

Army Form C. 2118.

1/4th Bn R Sco Fus

JULY 1919

Place	Date	Hour	Summary of Events and Information	Remarks and references to Appendices
HILDEN	6th		Church Parades: R.C as usual. Combined C of E & Pres: Service in Realschule HILDEN. Bn found Bde Duties. Guard found by 'A' Coy mounted at 1800 hours.	
—	7th		Advance party of 2 Off & representative of each unit in the Bn proceeded to BEDBURG to take over stores & Billets. Day spent by Bn in preparing for the move. As much loading as possible was done. A colour Party proceeded to PARIS on this date representing the Bn in the VICTORY march to take place on 14th July. Personnel. Kings Colour T/Capt J. MURRAY. M.C. Regtl. Colour a/Capt. W. A. MUIR. M.C. Escort No 8767 / RSM. T.C. TOOGOOD. M.C. No 43110 L/c Corpl. NESS. T. M.M. No 202229. a/Corpl COLLINS. G. D.C.M 53082 Pte BELL. D. M.M. This party left HILDEN by 13 30 train for COLOGNE.	
HILDEN - BEDBURG	8th	—	The Bn moved from HILDEN - BEDBURG. Paraded on Bn Parade Ground at 06 30 hrs. Entraining commenced 08.30 hrs. Arrived BEDBURG about 14.15 hrs via COLOGNE and DUREN met by Billeting party at Stn, each Coy marched off to billets. 'A' Coy in billets. 'B & D' Coys under canvas. 'C' Coy in Sugar Factory. Transport Lines in Sugar Factory Area taken over by 3rd Lowland Bde from 3rd Bde Light Division. Bn H Qrs located in a small school. 'B' Coy was detailed as Bde Loading Party and arrived about 21.30 in BEDBURG. Having marched from ROMMERSKIRCHEN. SAA & LG limbers proceeded by road crossing the RHINE by ferry at BENRATH.	
BEDBURG	9th		Day devoted to cleaning up and arrangements for messing etc.	

D. D. & L., London, E.C.
(a5340) Wt W5300/P713 750,000 5/18 Sch. 52a Forms/C2118/16.

Instructions regarding War Diaries and Intelligence Summaries are contained in F. S. Regs., Part II. and the Staff Manual respectively. Title pages will be prepared in manuscript.

WAR DIARY or ~~INTELLIGENCE SUMMARY.~~

(Erase heading not required.)

III

1/4th Royal Scots Fusiliers for JULY 1919

Army Form C. 2118.

Place	Date	Hour	Summary of Events and Information	Remarks and references to Appendices
BEDBURG	10th		Sick Parade 07.30 hours. Routine otherwise as usual. Bn paraded for a Route march at 09.30 hours Drill Order. Bn found Bde duties Gd for Bde H.Qrs found by 'B' Coy. An order was received from Bde pointing out that the water of river ERFT and tributaries were polluted with chemicals therefore to be no watering of horses etc.	
BEDBURG	11th		Routine as usual. Training under Coy arrangements. Each drawn for the four Fld Cashier at Duren by 2/Lt A.F.R. RICHARDSON. Vacancies for Spectators of Paris Victory March 1 off & 2 O.R. depart on 13th return on 15th.	
BEDBURG	12th		Weekly Inspection of billets by the Commanding Officer. M.O. weekly inspection. Bn Order No 282 states that 1/4th R.S.F. will find Bde H Qrs guard until further orders. This guard will be found automatically by Coy on duty for the day and will mount at same time as Bn Quarter Guard. Baths. – No 204508 L/Cpl WAYMATT 'B' Coy is appointed Bath Warden at the SCHLOSS. 2/Lt J.A.M. BRIGHT proceeded to HILDEN to complete handing over of Regimental Stores in HOTEL MONOPOL, to the 51st Rifle Bde.	
BEDBURG	13th		Church Parades and Routine as usual. 2 officers and 2 O.R. proceeded to PARIS as Spectators of the Victory March on 14th.	
BEDBURG	14th		The Colours of the 1/4th Bn were carried in the Victory March at PARIS on this day by Capt. J. MORRAY M.C. and Capt W.A. MUIR M.C. Training for all Coys. 09.30 – 12.00 Squad & Platoon Drill. Location Field East of River ERFT. NOTICE "All W.O's N.C.O's and men must be in billets by 22.30 hours unless on duty. (Ref. G.R.O. 2668. 20.4.19.)	

(10140) Wt W5300/P713 750,000 3/18 D. D. & L., London, E.C. E. 2688 Forms/C2118/10.

Instructions regarding War Diaries and Intelligence Summaries are contained in F. S. Regs., Part II. and the Staff Manual respectively. Title pages will be prepared in manuscript.

WAR DIARY

or

~~INTELLIGENCE SUMMARY.~~

(Erase heading not required.)

Army Form C. 2118.

IV JULY

1/4th Royal Scots Fusiliers
JULY 1919

Place	Date	Hour	Summary of Events and Information	Remarks and references to Appendices
BEDBURG	15th		Routine alterations in (i) First Post 22.15. Roll call 22.30. Last Post 22.45. Lights out 22.50. – Training. Bn carrying out fatigues. L.G. & Sig classes as usual. All Guards mounting at 17.15 daily, to Parade under RSM at 09.00 hours daily for 1 hour Guard Drill.	
BEDBURG	16th		Training. Bn Route March. BEDBURG – FLESCH – BERGHEIM & return to BEDBURG. Bde Riding School for Officers held on Bn Athletic Ground at 15.00 hours. T.O. provides 6 horses.	
BEDBURG	17th		Training. 'A' Coy 09.00 – 12.00 hrs. Squad & Platoon Drill, & Musketry. Location MEADOW East of the ERFT. – Hdqrs, Band, 'B' 'C' & 'D' Coys moved into the SCHLOSS at BEDBURG, vacating camp and Sugar Factory. The Corps Commander visited the Area on this date. Classification of Animals.	
BEDBURG	18th		Colour party returned from PARIS. Educational parades cancelled owing to lack of accommodation. Fatigue parties pitched marquees in Schloss grounds. Training under Coy arrangements. N.C.O.'s drill class. Bn alarm posts fixed. 'A' Marktplatz. 'B C D' Parade Ground in front of SCHLOSS.	
BEDBURG	19th		LONDON Peace March. This day was fixed by PARLIAMENT as a General Holiday throughout the Empire. Inter Coy sports took place, cricket football & Tennis. Transfers Lieut J. DALZIEL B – 'A' Coy 2/Lt W. Archer D – B' 2/Lt [illegible] – 'D' Coy. The Bn Orderly Officer to sleep in SCHLOSS from this date.	

(13340) Wt W3400/P713 750,000 3/18 D. D. & L. London, E.C. Sch. 52a Forms/C2118/16.

Instructions regarding War Diaries and Intelligence Summaries are contained in F. S. Regs., Part II. and the Staff Manual respectively. Title pages will be prepared in manuscript.

WAR DIARY
or
~~INTELLIGENCE SUMMARY.~~
(Erase heading not required.)

V JULY

Army Form C. 2118.

1/4 Royal Scots Fusiliers

Place	Date	Hour	Summary of Events and Information	Remarks and references to Appendices
BEDBURG	20th		Church Parades. C of E at 09.10 hours under orderly officer in Y.M.C.A. RC. & Pres. as usual. Routine as usual.	
BEDBURG	21st		Training. 'A' & 'B' Coys carried out Musketry on Bde Range at ERPRATH from 09.00 - 12.00 hours. B.G.C. 3rd Lowland Bde inspected the Bn Transport. Baths were allotted to coys between the hours of 10.00 and 16.30. Bn football team played the team selected from Belgian Army of Occupation at NEUSS. Result RSF 2 goals. BELGIANS 0.	
BEDBURG	22nd		Training. Usual Educational Parades. N.C.O's Drill Class under the R.S.M. - F.G.C.M. the following, all of 1/4th R.Sco.Fus. were tried by F.G.C.M. which assembled in the Schloss BEDBURG at 10.30 hours. No 11048 Pte Morrison J. 'B' Coy. No 52737 Pte Rae W. 'D' Coy. 42594 Pte Dunbar W. 'B' Coy. 52554 Pte McLean J. 'C' Coy. Baths allotted to companies 10.00 - 12.00 hours.	
BEDBURG	23rd		Routine as usual for 'C' & 'D' Coys. Musketry on Bde Ranges 09.00 - 12.00 hrs. N.C.Os Drill Class. 'A' & 'B' Coys carried out training under Coy arrangements. OC Coys, CQMS & Coy clerks attended a lecture on the P & M.B. at NETTESHEIM. The Adjutant inspected Div. H.Qrs guard at 08.30 hrs. Guard found by A Coy.	
BEDBURG	24th		Usual Routine. Training. Bn Route March. Following wire received. "The Brigadier congratulates 1/4th R.S.F. on winning the cup in the Association Football match against the BELGIAN Army of Occupation at NEUSS yesterday." Extract from London Gazette 6th Supplement dated 4.7.19. Specially mentioned ... Despatches of 16th March 1919. Dunsmuir W/Capt 1/4th Bn (T.F.)	

(6633) W. W5300/P713 750,000 1/19 D. D. & L. Forms C2118/14.

Instructions regarding War Diaries and Intelligence Summaries are contained in F. S. Regs., Part II. and the Staff Manual respectively. Title pages will be prepared in manuscript.

WAR DIARY
or
~~INTELLIGENCE SUMMARY.~~ 1/4th R. Sco Fus
(Erase heading not required.)

VI JULY 1919 Army Form C. 2118.

Place	Date	Hour	Summary of Events and Information	Remarks and references to Appendices
BEDBURG	24th		Continued from V Gitt. Major (a/Lt Col. now Temp Lt Col) C Commdg 1/4th Bn (T.F.). McEwan T/Major J. A. atts 1/5th Bn (T.F) now atts 1/4th Bn (T.F. Yuille. QrMr & Major. D. 1/4th Bn (T.F) Day. 34840. Sgt A. 2nd Bn atts 1/4th RSF. Galbraith 41222. Pte Now L/Cpl 2nd Bn atts 1/4th (TF Bn): Martin 200737 Pte a/L/Cpl. 1/4th Bn (T.F). Moffat 40536 Pte G. 1st Bn atts 1/4th Bn (T.F). Richardson 200988 Pte J. 1/4th Bn (T.F). Sorley 23516 Pte J. 2nd Bn atts 1/4 (T.F). Wilson 200727 Pte (a/Cpl) A 1/4th Bn T.F. atts 155th L.T.M. Bty. The following sentences of FGCM were promulgated: No 11048. J. Morrison 12 mos I.H.L. —: 41594 Pte W. DUNBAR 9 months IHL. 52584 Pte McKean 56 Days F.P. No 2 —: No 52737 Pte W. RAE. Forfeits 21 days Pay.	
BEDBURG	25th		Usual Routine. Training for those not attending Educational Classes and on [illegible] arrangements. Usual Bn weekly Educational Classes. N.C.Os class under the RSM. Lecture 09-30 - 10-11 on "War Savings Certificates" by Major Wade. R.F.A. L/Cpl Kennedy appointed Hon Sec & Sgt [illegible] Galbraith Hon Treasurer of Bn War Savings Association; F.G.C.M following were tried by FGCM. 19548 Pte FARMER H 'B' Coy. 41555 Pte Sawers H. 'A' Coy. Compliment. "G.O.C Lowland Div. per II Corps "As the Division under your command has now left the Corps I shall be glad if you will convey to all ranks my thanks and appreciation of the work they have done in the BERGRATH-HERZOGEN-SOLINGEN area. The Division has kept up the reputation [illegible] to them by 9th Division [illegible] duty has been excellent	

D. D. & L., London, E.C. (19210) Wt W5300/P713 750,000 3/18 E 2688 Forms/C2118/16.

Instructions regarding War Diaries and Intelligence Summaries are contained in F. S. Regs., Part II. and the Staff Manual respectively. Title pages will be prepared in manuscript.

WAR DIARY
or
~~INTELLIGENCE~~ SUMMARY.
(Erase heading not required.)

VII. JULY

1/4th R. Sco. Fus.

Army Form C. 2118.

Place	Date	Hour	Summary of Events and Information	Remarks and references to Appendices
BEDBURG	25th		Ankton for VI. "It is with great regret that I leave the Division no longer in 2nd Corps (Sgd) C. Jacob. Lieut Gen. Commdg II Corps.	
BEDBURG	26th		Usual C.O's billet inspection:- M.O's weekly Inspection. Appointment Lieut G. Foote 1/5th R. Bn attd 1/4th Bn to be A/Capt whilst commanding a Coy. from 28th 1919. Authority 3rd Lowland Bde. A.S.C. 1/680. 28.7.19.	
BEDBURG.	27th		Church Parades as usual. Routine as usual. Informed by Bde that C in C would inspect Bn on Tuesday 29th at 1100 hrs.	
BEDBURG	28th		Routine as usual. The day was devoted to cleaning up and preparing for C in C's Inspection. 18.00 hours Lecture by Major A.P. Bowen M.C. on the Naval Raid at ZEEBRUGGE.	
BEDBURG	29th	–	Routine. Reveille 06.15 hours. Breakfasts 07.15 hours. Coy Commdrs Billet Inspection 08.05 Bn Parade 08.45. Dress Belt & Side arms. 11.30 Educational Examinations. Trained N.C.Os and Junior Hourly parades as usual under the R.S.M. 10.30 hrs. Signalling & Gas classes from 10.30 hours. P.T. Parade under Lieut G. Robertson 10.30 hrs. C.O. billet Inspection 10.15 hrs. Inspection by General Officer Commanding in Chief British Army of the Rhine Gen Sir William Robertson. Lieut Col C. [illegible] returned from U.K. Leave. Extract from Bn Routine Orders of 29th. "The Commanding Officer was highly satisfied with the General Turn out & cleanliness of billets on the Inspection by the General Officer Commanding in Chief British Army of the Rhine this morning, he wishes to congratulate all concerned.	

D. D. & L., London, E.C.
(10340) W1 W5300/P713 750,000 3/18 E 2688 Forms/C2118/16.

Army Form C. 2118.

Instructions regarding War Diaries and Intelligence Summaries are contained in F. S. Regs., Part II. and the Staff Manual respectively. Title pages will be prepared in manuscript.

WAR DIARY
or
~~INTELLIGENCE SUMMARY.~~
(Erase heading not required.)

VIII JULY
1/4th R. Sco. Fus.

Place	Date	Hour	Summary of Events and Information	Remarks and references to Appendices
BEDBURG	30th		Routine as usual except that dinners were at 12.00 hours. There was no training or other duty owing to the Bn Athletic Sports taking place. Coys supplied fatigue parties for preparation of Sports Field. Sports commenced 13.00 hours. Sports commenced at 13.00 hours and resulted in a win on points for 'C' Coy.	
BEDBURG	31st		Bn. Training. Bn Route March 09.30 – 1200 hours. Fatigues.	

J.A. McEwen.
Major. Commanding
1/4th Bn Royal Scots Fusiliers

BEDBURG. 31st July 1919.

D. D. & L., London, E.C.
(10340) Wt W5300/P713 750,000 3/18 E 2688 Forms/C2118/16.

I

3rd Low

Instructions regarding War Diaries and Intelligence Summaries are contained in F. S. Regs., Part II. and the Staff Manual respectively. Title pages will be prepared in manuscript.

WAR DIARY
or
~~INTELLIGENCE SUMMARY.~~
(Erase heading not required.)

Army Form C. 2118.

7th Bn Royal Scots [illegible]
August 1919. [illegible]

Place	Date	Hour	Summary of Events and Information	Remarks and references to Appendices
BEDBORG	1st		Routine as usual. Training [illegible]. Fatigue Parties were supplied by the Bn for the purpose of [illegible] the camp recently vacated by "B" and "D" Coys. [illegible] Fatigue parties on Sports Field. Issue of clothing to Coys. 2/Lt. F. T. BLANCKENBORG proceeded this day to join CHINESE LABOUR Corps for duty on Transfer.	[illegible]
BEDBORG	2nd		Routine as usual. Lecture by Dr. Alan [illegible] B.L. on "[illegible] in [illegible]" at 10.00 hours in the SCHLOSS BEDBORG. All men available were present. Usual N.C.O.s Inspection Weekly. Bn Imprest account was closed on 31st July. Pay & Mess Book System commenced on 1st August 1919.	[illegible]
BEDBORG	3rd		Routine and Church Parades as usual.	[illegible]
BEDBORG	4th		Declared a General Holiday [illegible] Training was suspended for the day. Sports were held. Baths allotted to the Bn [illegible] Concert Party gave a concert in YMCA BEDBORG at 18.00 hours.	[illegible]
BEDBORG	5th		Routine as usual. Bn weekly Education Classes. N.C.O.s class under the RSM. [illegible] Lt. Col. [illegible] took over the command of the Bn vice Major J. A. McEwen [illegible] on vacating Temporary Command of 3rd Lowland Bde.	[illegible]
BEDBORG	6th		Routine as usual. Duty and [illegible] fatigues. Bn paraded by Coys for [illegible] Inspection by Divisional [illegible] Training under Coy arrangements. Lieut. [illegible] M.C. reported to ENGINEER in Chief RHINE Army for [illegible]	[illegible]
BEDBORG	7th		Routine. Reveille 06.15 hours. [illegible] 08.00 hours. 7 OCM [illegible] at Bn H.Q. for [illegible] of following Pte. McLelland and Browne to the [illegible] [illegible] The [illegible] was cancelled by Bde. Wire.	[illegible]

C. D. D. & L., London, E.C. (10310) Wt W5300/P713 750,000 3/18 E 2688 Forms/C2118/16.

24.B
5 sheets

Instructions regarding War Diaries and Intelligence Summaries are contained in F. S. Regs., Part II. and the Staff Manual respectively. Title pages will be prepared in manuscript.

Sheet. V

WAR DIARY
or
~~INTELLIGENCE SUMMARY.~~
(Erase heading not required.)

1/4th Bn Royal Scots Fusiliers

AUGUST 1919

Germany

Army Form C. 2118.

Place	Date	Hour	Summary of Events and Information	Remarks and references to Appendices
BEDBURG	8th		Routine as usual. Bi-weekly Education Classes. Training 10.00 – 11.00. N.C.O's class under R.S.M. Signalling Classes under the Signalling Officer 1000 hours. 'C' Coy found a Canteen Guard for [illegible] Canteen at DÜREN 1 NCO and 12 O.R. [illegible] Transfer Lieut G.L. [illegible] M.C. transferred to 'D' Coy from this date. 2/Lt J. REID took over temporary command of H.Q. Ser Coy in absence of Lieut J. CARNAN M.C. on 14 days leave. Full Dress [illegible] to be withdrawn from all troops forthwith and stored Regimentally. Authy G.R.O. 3264 dated 4/8/19. Warning order re Inspection by Army Commander on 12th inst at HARFF.	jmm
BEDBURG	9th		Billet Inspection by C.O. commencing 10.00 hours with H.Q. Ser Coy. M.O's weekly inspection 11.00 hours. Training. R.S.M's parade 09.30 hours. Evening [illegible] C.O. [illegible] Bn football field. Education Results of Preliminary Elementary Examination 'A' Coy 49% passed 51% failed. 'B' 62% passed 38% failed. 'C' Coy 32% passed 68% failed. 'D' 44% passed 56%. Highest Individual Results:- 1st No 49858 Private SPENCE J. 'A' Coy. 2nd No 41578 Private Smith W. 'B' Coy. 3rd 352725 Pte ANDREWS A. 'B' Coy. Cricket Match 1/4th R.S.F. v M.T. A.S.C. Coy. Result M.T. A.S.C. 61 runs 1/4 R.S.F. 17 runs.	jmm
BEDBURG	10th		Routine and Church Parades as usual. The special parade for Army Commander's visit cancelled by Bde Wire. This refers to the Parade at HARFF on 12th inst.	jmm
BEDBURG	11th		Routine as usual. 09.00 hours R.S.M's Parade. 10.30 – 11.00 Monthly kit inspection all deficiencies to be made up as soon as possible. Baths allotted to Coys on this date. Scheme commencing on this date, [illegible] Mon. & Thurs for their [illegible]; [illegible] Book System at No 9 FRIEDERICH WILHELM STRASSE. BEDBURG. A Tennis Tournament for Officers held at BEDBURG.	jmm

D. D. & L., London, E.C.
(10540) Wt W5300/P713 750,000 3/18 E 2688 Forms/C2118/16.

Instructions regarding War Diaries and Intelligence Summaries are contained in F. S. Regs., Part II. and the Staff Manual respectively. Title pages will be prepared in manuscript.

WAR DIARY
or
~~INTELLIGENCE~~ SUMMARY. of 1/4th Btn. Royal Scots Fusiliers. August 1919 Germany

(Erase heading not required.)

Sheet III

Army Form C. 2118.

Place	Date	Hour	Summary of Events and Information	Remarks and references to Appendices
Bedburg	12th		Routine as usual Bi-weekly Education Classes – 2nd Examination for Active Service Schools Certificates Elementary Training – Under Company arrangements, for those not attending Education Signalling Classes.	
Bedburg	13th		Routine as usual Training Musketry "A & B" Coys on Range. "C & D" under Coy Arrangements – Signalling Classes. Special parade re Army Councils visit cancelled by wire. Divisional Guard found by "B" Coy was inspected by A/Adjt at 08 30 hours. Audit Board assembled to audit accounts of Sergts. Mess, & Band fund. Pres. Capt Foot, members Lt JJ Campbell, 2/Lt A A J Caban	
Bedburg	14th		In view of the fact that Lt-Col Gibb received orders to join 2nd Btn R S Fus at Aldershot forthwith the Brig General granted the Battn a whole holiday on this date. Command Capt W R Muir MC, in the absence of Maj McEwen on UK Leave, temporarily assumed Command of the Btn. vice Lt Col Gibb who proceeded to UK on this date. Lecture on The Palestine Campaign by Rev. C W R Wheeler in Schloss	
Bedburg	15th		Training Bi weekly Education Classes. Lecture to Apprentices by Lieut Carre, 0900 to 1000 hrs. British Empire Leave Party proceeded as Brigade Party. Torchlight Tattoo at Niedegger. Concert Party in Y M C A.	
Bedburg	16th		Routine as usual weekly Billet Inspection by C.O. followed by Medical Inspection	
Bedburg	17th		Routine as usual. Usual Church Parades C of E & R Cs No Presbyterian parade	
Bedburg	18th		Education Examination for Active Service Certificates. Court of Enquiry Capt Foote Lt D. Munro Lt JJ Campbell All O Rs of Duty Scheme joined for Service before 1/1/19 eligible for Demobilisation	

D. D. & L., London, E.C. (10340) Wt W5300/P713 750,000 3/18 E 2688 Forms/C2118/16.

Instructions regarding War Diaries and Intelligence Summaries are contained in F. S. Regs., Part II. and the Staff Manual respectively. Title pages will be prepared in manuscript.

WAR DIARY
or
~~INTELLIGENCE SUMMARY.~~
(Erase heading not required.)

Sheet IV
of 1/4th Royal Scots Fusiliers
August 1919 Germany

Army Form C. 2118.

Place	Date	Hour	Summary of Events and Information	Remarks and references to Appendices
Bedburg	19th		Routine as usual. Major McEwen assumed command of the Battn vice Capt W. S. Moir. Training "A + B" Coys Musketry on Bdge Range "C + D" under Company arrangements. A Saluting Parade at first Opportunity. 2/Lt Austin admitted to 36th C.C.S.	
Bedburg	20th		Routine as usual - Training "C + D" Coys Musketry on Bdge Range. "A + B" Coys Tactical Instruction (as a Drill) on Battn Parade Ground. 5 off + 100 O.R. of "A" Coy to proceed to **HERBESTHAL** to relieve 1/8 Sco. Rif. "B" Coy to detail 1 N.C.O. + 8 O.R. to ~~relief~~ 1/8 relieve at Control Post, STEENSTRASSE. Officers "Order Book" instituted in the Battn. F. G. C. M. convened. Pres Maj. McKinlay 1/8 S.R. members Capt G.A Foote Lieut J.J. Campbell Prosecutor Lieut A. BARCLAY. All O.Rs in future to wear Identity Discs.	
Bedburg	21st		Routine as usual. Training. Adjutants Parade 9-10. 10-30 - 12. Extended Order + Coy Drill. Iron Rations to be re-issued to Units. Civilians permitted to circulate from 04.00 hrs to 24.00 hrs.	
Bedburg	22nd		Routine as usual. Education parade as usual under Orderly Officer at 08.45 hrs. British Soldiers permitted to assist in Local Harvesting of Volunteers + Paid for work. F.G.C.M. convened. Pres Maj McKinlay. Members Capt G.A Foote + 2/Lt Hopper 1/8 S.R.	
Bedburg	23rd		Routine as usual. Weekly Billet Inspection.	
Bedburg	24th		Routine as usual. Church Parades. R.Cs under 2/Lt Thomson at 10.45 hrs. C of Es under 2/Lt A P Main at 10-20 hrs. Presbyterians under Lt McIndoe at 11.00 hrs.	
Bedburg	25th		Routine as usual. Training "B" Coy on Bdge Range "C + D" Coys Tactical Instruction 0900 - 1200 hrs. In future all men to carry 60 rds Ammunition.	
Bedburg	26th		Routine as usual. Training. Adjutants Parade 08.30 - 09.30. Education parade for all coys 09.30 to 12.30 hrs. All ORs not on Education Saluting parade under R.S.M. 09-30 - 11.45 hrs. 11-45 hrs 12.15 hrs Lecture by Adjutant Inf. Drill Chapter III. 2/Lt Cunningham placed on sick list.	

D. D. & L., London, E.C.
(10340) Wt W5300/P713 750,000 3/18 E 2688 Forms/C2118/16.

Instructions regarding War Diaries and Intelligence Summaries are contained in F. S. Regs., Part II. and the Staff Manual respectively. Title pages will be prepared in manuscript.

WAR DIARY

or

INTELLIGENCE SUMMARY. of 1/4th Royal Scots Fusiliers

(*Erase heading not required.*)

Sheet V

Army Form C. 2118.

August 1919 GERMANY

Place	Date	Hour	Summary of Events and Information	Remarks and references to Appendices
Bedburg	27th		Routine as usual. Battalion parade for Musketry practice. Competitions to be fired	
Bedburg	28th		Routine as usual. Adjutants parade 08·30 hrs to 09·30 hrs. C.O's parade Route March at 10·00 hrs.	
Bedburg	29th		Routine as usual. Adjutants parade 08·30 hrs to 09·15 hrs. Education parades as usual at 09·30 hrs. Men not on education at Disposal of O.C. Companies.	
Bedburg	30th		Usual weekly billet inspection by Commanding Officer. Followed by weekly Medical inspection. Instructions for preparation for move to U.K.	
Bedburg	31st		Routine as usual. Church parades as usual. R.C's under 2/Lt Harrison for service in Bedburg 09·15 hrs. Presbyterians etc under Maj. McEwen for service in Y.M.C.A. at 11·30 hrs.	

J. A. McEwen
Major Lieut.-Colonel,
Commdg. 1/4th Bn. Royal Scots Fusiliers

D. D. & L., London, E.C.
(10340) Wt W5300/P713 750,000 3/18 E 2688 Forms/C2118/16.

www.ingramcontent.com/pod-product-compliance
Lightning Source LLC
Chambersburg PA
CBHW081457160426
43193CB00013B/2518